RAISING THE TENTS

The publication of this book was supported with grants from the National Endowment for the Arts Advancement Program, The Lannan Foundation, and the Oregon Arts Commission.

Cover art "Dancing in the Thorns of the Thistle" by Kira Corser
Cover design by Carolyn Sawtelle and Micki Reaman
Book design and layout by Cheryl McLean and Micki Reaman

CALYX Books are distributed to the trade by Consortium Book Sales & Distribution, Inc., St. Paul, MN, 1-800-283-3572. CALYX Books are also available through major library distributors, jobbers, and most small press distributors including: Airlift, Bookpeople, Inland Book Co., Pacific Pipeline, and Small Press Distribution. For personal orders or other information write: CALYX Books, PO Box B, Corvallis, OR 97339, (503) 753-9384. FAX (503) 753-0515.

∞

The paper in this book meets the guidelines for permanence and durability of the Committee on Production Guidelines for Book Longevity of the Council on Library Resources and the minimum requirements of the American National Standard for the Permanence of Paper for Printed Library Materials Z38.48-1984.

Library of Congress Cataloging-in-Publication Data

Adler, Frances Payne,
      Raising the tents / Frances Payne Adler
                p.   cm.
      ISBN 0-934971-34-X (alk.paper) : $19.95. — ISBN 0-934971-33-1
      (pbk.) : $9.95.
        1. Women—Poetry. I. Title
      PS3551.D594R35 1993   93-650
      8ll'.54—dc20   CIP

Printed in the U.S.A.

RAISING THE TENTS

FRANCES PAYNE ADLER

CALYX BOOKS □ CORVALLIS, OREGON

Acknowledgements

Thanks to the National Endowment for the Arts and the Copley Foundation for the grants that enabled me to complete some of this work.

Acknowledgement is made to the following publications in which these poems were previously published: "Friendly Fire," *Women's Review of Books*, Vol. X, No. 5, February 1993; "The Women Ago," "Speakbody," and excerpt from "Drumskin," in *When The Bough Breaks: Pregnancy and the Legacy of Addiction* (NewSage Press, 1993); "Telephone to The Dead," *Exquisite Corpse*, Louisiana State University, No. 33, Fall 1991; "Ruth," an earlier version appeared in *Shirim*, Hillel, Los Angeles, Vol. II, Spring 1983, and was reprinted in *Blood To Remember: American Poets on the Holocaust* (Texas Tech University Press, 1991); "Riding The Eye" and "Simply," *CALYX, A Journal of Art and Literature by Women*, Vol. 13, No. 1, Winter 1990-91; "Switchback" and "Begot," *Bridges*, New Jewish Agenda, Seattle, Vol. 1, No. 1, Spring 1990; "Woman, Diaspora," *Daughters of Sarah*, Daughters of Sarah Press, Chicago, March/April 1990; "Wood Floor Rising," *Hayden's Ferry Review*, Arizona State University, Issue 5, Fall 1989; "That Act of Violence," *Women and Politics* (Haworth Press, 1989); "Don't Ever Tell," *No Street Poets Voice*, Caernarvon Press, San Diego, CA, Vol. 7, No. 12, December 1989; "Joshua" and "Back," *Struggle To Be Borne*, a collaborative book of poetry and photography about childbirth and poverty, with photographs by Kira Corser (San Diego State University Press, San Diego, CA, 1988); "Los Desaparecidos," *State and Local Politics: A*

Political Economic Approach, West Publishing, St. Paul, MN, January 1988; "Mother Tongue" and "Underground," *Pacific Review,* San Diego State University, Winter 1986; "Signals," *Centennial Review,* Michigan State University, Vol. XXX, No. 4, Fall 1986; "Bag Woman" and "Where," *Home Street Home,* a collaborative book of poetry and photography about homelessness, with photographs by Kira Corser, San Diego, CA, 1984.

Grateful acknowledgement is made to the following for permission to reprint: The lines from "Planetarium" and "Twenty-One Love Poems: VII" are reprinted from *THE FACT OF A DOORFRAME, Poems Selected and New, 1950-1984,* by Adrienne Rich, by permission of the author and W.W. Norton & Company, Inc. Copyright © 1984 by Adrienne Rich. Copyright © 1975,1978 by W.W. Norton & Company, Inc. Copyright © 1981 by Adrienne Rich; Excerpt by Helen Epstein from *Children of the Holocaust,* by permission of the author; Excerpt by Raphael Patai from *The Hebrew Goddess* (Wayne State University Press, Detroit, Michigan, 1990), originally published as "The Goddess Asherah" in *Journal of Near Eastern Studies,* January-April 1965, Chapter One; Susan Griffin, *Woman and Nature: The Roaring Inside Her,* Copyright © 1978 by Susan Griffin, Reprinted by permission of HarperCollins Publishers Inc.; Excerpt by H.D. from "Flowering of the Rod," *Trilogy,* Copyright © 1982, The Estate of Hilda Doolittle, by permission of New Directions Pub. Corp.

for Kira, my sister-traveler

CONTENTS

INTRODUCTION

Telephone to the Dead

I. BEGOT

II. SPEAKBODY

Who went in the way before you to search you out a place to pitch your tents...

— Deuteronomy 1:33

INTRODUCTION

Telephone to the Dead

Toward the end of the 20th century, the bone phone came into use.
A large receiver made of sanded femur
caught the frequency to the dead.
You could only use it at night. You couldn't call collect.
Sometimes you might get a busy signal:
someone other than you was calling the same dead.
It was found that women called their mothers, men their fathers.
It was said that when you finally got through,
you might find that nothing came out of your mouth.
You might even break out in a sweat.
The only questions that could be transmitted
were those between the generations
that had never before been asked.

ONE:
BEGOT

...blighted elms, sick rivers, massacres...that desecration of ourselves...
Adrienne Rich, "Twenty-One Love Poems, VII"

Begot

I wonder if they knew they got more than six million, knew the gas
would seep through generations, three so far and where from here,
this table, white cloth, black wine, some bread, a room the other side
of the earth, and still the gas: her husband, forty-one years red in his face
neck veined like a penis ready to shoot point blank

Crossing

Did the Jews not assume a role that was
*   inappropriate for them?*
Did they not perhaps deserve to be put in their
*   place?*

       —Nov. 10, 1988, Philipp Jenninger,
       president, West German Parliament
       Bonn, 50th anniversary, *Kristallnacht*

Early 1940s, on the border

I.   "When's Aunt Ruth coming?"
       "Soon, David."
       "But when."

       "You over there, you better keep that kid
       quiet."

       "Sshhh."
       "My fingers are numb."
       "I said, sshhh."
       "They feel like sticks."

       "Where *is* she, Anna."

       "Poppa."
       "She'll come when she comes. We promised
       her we'd wait."
       "Poppa."

       "Will you shut that kid up?"

"Get away from that window. Get
down. Damn it, I said, *get down.*"
"All I did was look to see if she..."
"Sit *still.*"

"Where *is* your sister, Anna."
"Soon. She'll be here."
"We have to leave."
"I'm not crossing without her."
"We have to get out of here."
"I'm waiting for Ruth."

"Poppa, I hear someone."

*"Do I have to reach over there and
do it myself?"*

"David, shut up."
"Max. Don't."
"Anna, stop that crying."
"Poppa, my fingers."
"Oy Got, Davey..."

II.   *She'd make a run
for it as soon as
the guard turned*

*she couldn't keep
her eyes off the hut
as if the line between it*

and her
were a bridge and if
she turned away
it would collapse

everything beginning
to blur, the roof, the
ground she'd covered, mud
under her skin, the jeep hey,
you, the boots, the rot in her
throat, mud inside the trees

one, two, the roof, the mold
the wood in her head pounding,
the broken window an
eye streaking
the ground she'd
covered, one two five

seven maybe fifty pine,
juniper, spruce, green
turned gray, and the air

precise, yes, marking
hairs in her nose,
her chest locking to ice,

rain for days, coming up
in rushes, liquid bats,
maggots

she stamped out one then
another, they bloated, sawdust
on her boots. The hut, small, a broken

doghouse, really, first time she
saw it with David years ago
under branches looks like

it's crying, Aunt Ruth,
he'd said, they were counting
trees years before all this started

how many feet of lumber
crossing one kilometer east
of the border how many

songs do you know
Dave

That Act of Violence

For years it lay in an iron box buried so deep inside me that I was never sure
what it was.... I had caught glimpses...
                —Helen Epstein, *Children of the Holocaust*

I.

in the name of love
he counted to five and married her, they laughed,
because she filled him and it was time ending school to find a wife

and, in the name of love, they laughed,
she left her father's house
his rum moving the rooms around *hold your tongue girl*

she slipped on ice in *peau de soie* shoes he held
her arm and smiled for the camera *one more over here*

in the name of love
he called her *squirrel* and when the kids came,
he stopped—

in the name of love
he called her *dummy* and when she said
don't he put arms around her *can't you take a joke*

in the name of love during the war
he'd climbed the ghetto wall and back three times
telling lies

the sweat of his back an open pit
uniforms at airports border crossings police *I'll do the talking*

in the name of love
he yelled at the boy, blue shoulders stretched for breath
you ran out without a jacket you made yourself sick

in the name of love
just wait he told the girl bent over books
you'll end up waiting tables

in the name of the money he made, *I deserve* he said
breakfast on the table two eggs over, coffee toast light

II.

she thought of moving
the room around the way she hadn't done since she was a kid

close the door push dresser bed bookcase

she didn't know why mornings
she held the boy and the girl too tightly

or why in the name of love she closed the door went back to school

or why when she came home climbing the high wires
in her head and new books in the name of love he said

now let me tell you what reality is

and when words came to her in the name of love she wrote
"he called her *dummy* and when she said *don't...*"

he called her *dangerous* in the name of love *writing lies*

he pulled the phone wires when she wrote "for all those years
she drove her kids to baseball she could have been any one of us"

Riding the Eye

Maybe, if she didn't have adobe walls between her
and 70-mile-an-hour calls, collect calls crazing the wires
from whatever phones he found to serve his need, maybe
if she didn't have baseball bats, Louisville Slugger High Velocity
Cupped and Balanced Number Eights,
tucked between her bed and the wall, maybe then
she would let bones seep from her feet, knobs tighten her back,
maybe then it would rise mercury to her tongue,
I am scared. The day she left, the day of the split, in dust light
behind the door hiding from him, his hands in her head, the fine snips,
the knife of his words. *I have to get out of here*, she said
to herself, *out*, his back flat to the door, his need turning the bolt.
Shit, her gut could've been sheets twisted from wind from where
to what. *Have I ever*, he said. Her suitcase, the lock, the damn lock
stuck, a sweater, some books and the cat *I'll find you*
his hands *stop* to her windshield left at the corner four lights the freeway
and out to the night north through the storm, waves gusting the west,
wind blanking lights to the east and south he was calling, turning
and calling above her head, wires harpooning her new number,
calling her brother *she has to come back,* her sister, her friends,
*collect call from David, will you accept, collect from Gabriel will you
accept, from Roberto, Steven, Sebastian, Juan, collect from John Francis,
Andre, Benjamin, Malcolm, Dominic, collect, will you accept,*
will you let this man back into your house, your skin, your air, your dust,
will you accept at four in the morning the call *I'm three blocks away*
and the pounding the door and the pounding

Night Rider

Someone I lost.
She fell down between the cracks of
this year and last
and in a small voice floating away said
don't try to find me

I grew thin wouldn't eat waiting
for her to call and in the length of night, yes
calling me long distance asking
why I'm not there giving directions

Divorce And

for Sybil

I wake, the last months a knife in my back,
its bladetip dares my sudden breath. I watch the ceiling unravel
to electrical wire, studs, old shouts in the gridwork.
Walls split under my touch. I put my finger in,
wet, translucent, tiny grapes growing from it. Outside
the steps, I find my mom, dead for fifteen years,
hosing the sidewalk. These dogs, she says.
Will you be here in time for tea?

Bag Woman

Accidents arrive slow and without an appointment.
I barely see a car arrange itself into the metal
that was the engine of my car. Just its sound:
like twigs underfoot cracking the night open.
People gather to watch the repair truck disentangle
one car from another. They don't see a woman
sitting alone near a wall, a steel shopping cart
filled with all she owns. I can't look and I can't look away.
She has wrapped her face in green garbage bags.
She believes as I did as a child when I covered my eyes,
she has disappeared. Like the wrecked cars,
I could at any moment accidentally be like her. I look away.
The repair truck parked beside me
isn't piled high with danger markers, no red triangles
ready to be placed around sudden holes in the road
or behind a line of cars backed up
as if to say this route closed.

The Women Ago

I am white blood curtains tracking the night for those who know me
I set out backwards from morning through holes drugged with blankets
I talk with voices carrying garbage out to burn, eyes shuffle behind glass
Behind roads, the white lines are broken, I keep wanting to pass

I am here, face me faceless, you live in my name

Where

There is no hunger in America.

> —Edwin Meese,
> U.S. Attorney General,
> January 1984

*There is no documentable evidence
of rampant hunger in this country.*

> —Presidential Task
> Force, March 1984

This is not the Depression:
People wait in line
for food, jammed
into a walkway
outside the church.
A sign at the curb
says *Stop.*
Another says
No Left Turn.
A woman sits.
On a ledge beneath
the stained glass window
she takes up little space.
Masking tape
holds her jeans together.
Hunger, she says,
has made it difficult
to talk. It has
hit her in the stomach
like a fist
that shatters glass.
It has cut

the height of her glance
the boom of her voice.
She is slowly being erased.
The roll of her blanket,
her small sac, a comb,
hold her together.
She even welcomes the lice.
They make her scratch,
remind her she is still here.

Gravity Reversed

for Sybil

On the day gravity is reversed,
pots that hang from the kitchen ceiling
turn upright and fill themselves
with everything I ever cooked.
Chairs repeat exact conversations of table talk.

Even the clocks are affected,
roll backwards. Photo albums
lining the living room walls
turn upright the years since my birth,
click my mother back to life.
She climbs down from bookshelves,
dressed in summer cotton,
looks in pots for something to eat.

She fills the halls,
different aged versions of herself.
Twenty-four at the piano, in satin, in love.
Forty in the flowered chair
watching through windows.
Fifty-nine writing at her desk.
Black has slipped from her hair
to pockets under her eyes.

There are some things
even gravity can't unloose.
Momma, I say, *talk to me.*
She smiles for the camera.
I bend over her, watch her write.

Don't Ever Tell

I.   The small boy plays Follow-the-Crack
        in front of the tomatoes at Safeway.
        His mother, skittish, tells him to stop.
        I stand beside them, picking squash.
        She looks over her shoulder.
        The boy's eyes follow hers, become slits.
        I've never seen the boy, his mother before.
        I've seen them before.
        Later, behind me at the check-out,
        the father's with them. He unloads
        the beer, the Tide, sausage, bourbon,
        bread. She adds ice cream.
        No, you can't get that, he tells his wife,
        how many times do I have to tell you.
        Hairs on the back of my neck.
        The woman lowers her eyes. Her neck
        is scratched, her hair needs a wash.
        She takes a Better Homes from the rack,
        turns the pages. The boy hangs upside
        down on the metal bar. The father scowls
        at him, the webbed lines on his nose, flare,
        redden, *how many times,* he says, pulls him
        down by the arm, shoves him into the magazine rack.
        The boy lowers his eyes, gray, looks up at him
        through eyelashes. His shoulders hang. *I wasn't doing*
        anything, he says. He looks at his mom, she looks away.
        The boy steps back, raises his elbow over his eyes,
        blocks the arm only a second. We all know what's coming.

II.   The backs of my legs stick to the seat plastic
on the ride in from the airport. Steve tells me
they found him on the floor beside the television,
his bottle of Smirnoff on the table. He was holding
a can of peanuts. They were in his hands, his pant cuffs,
his hair. My fingers sweat in my brother's.
I watch the palm trees line the street.
The ferns at the top, too relaxed, obscene in their ease.

The hospital's second floor makes me gag.
Comes off the wall like fresh paint and makes me gag.
Look, I was a nurse years ago and the smell did it to me
then too, the smell of bodies losing their shit
and I can't do this, my father's in there
and he's losing his shit and I'm not going in the room.

He's sitting in a chair staring at his feet.
His green eyes have gone gray.
His hair like feathers on the pillow.
He's strapped into the chair
and I think how many times
have I strapped people into chairs,
kept them from slipping.
But this is my father in there
and all I can think of is his leather razor strap
hanging behind the bathroom door at home.
The times he took it down, bent over my brother,
I wasn't doing anything, and closed the door.
I'd run to my room close the door cover my ears

and yell stop, please somebody make him stop.
But I could still hear the sound behind teeth
of Steve not crying out. Mornings he my father
would mix lather in a shaving mug, run the blade
across the strap, back again, lean into the mirror,
pull his face sideways.

He stares at his feet like chess pieces waiting
his next move and I say *hi Dad.* He looks at his feet.
Steve is rolling a Kleenex ball in his hands, shredding it.
The years between us slip from his face.
Don't ever tell anyone, promise, he'd said to me
the day he'd shot a bird with his BB gun.
He'd propped a tin can on top of the fence
and aimed at a robin instead. I was five, he was twelve,
and my Stevie had shot a bird. It hung in my head
years like some wet tarp that wouldn't dry.
I remember the day Dad perched on the bed,
watched Stevie finger the gun, clinked the cubes
in his glass, warned him not to aim at people.
I stand in the room, look at my father, my brother
bent over him. I can hear the bird stop.

Sybil

Momma, I hear you in your housedress
mix the wrong words to songs, see you hide
his razor strap. I'm trying to reach you, Sybil.
I walk back through the smell of onion and garlic you cut
the afternoon you left. *I'm not ready to die,*
you'd said, slipping the ropes of sleep,
your eyelids friable as ventricles
under my mouth. And from the sleep before death,
your thin *not ready* hangs fifteen years
like mirrors fogged with caught breath.

Wood Floor Rising

It's the smell of rain, the mix of water
and wood shutters. Floor wax
on our fingers, soup about done on the stove.
You ask why I pause, retreat from photographs
we've spread across the bed, the afternoon.
You sense the photo not taken.

I was a kid, just a kid.
My teachers couldn't understand
why a sudden pool appeared beneath my desk.
Years later, I still cringe,
the smell of urine wetting wood floor rising,
there are some things so difficult to tell you.

I was old, in the fourth grade, how old
are you in the fourth grade, nine?
Nine years old, I was no kid.
Beneath my desk the wet would stink,
the stink would rise,
and they would laugh.
How could they know, how could I tell them,
there are some things so difficult to say.

How could they know, I didn't know
the bottles my father drank, bottles
bloated him with rage he spit
at me. I didn't know it was the beer.
It was always something I did
or didn't do. *Sit up straight, look at me,*
why is this wrong, what did I tell you
to do, why is this not done, look at me,
I said, look at me. There are some things
that are so difficult.

How could I know everyone was not like this.
It seemed he had some right.
I would do just as I was told,
then there would be no rage.
How could I know the rage was endless,
the bottles endless, no way to end the rage.
I would have to end myself. I would disappear,
make myself invisible, never
call attention to myself, never
put my hand up in class
ask to leave the room, never
thinking of the pool, why were they
all looking at me *look at me*
I said, look at me. There are some things.

There are some things I have to tell you.
How it has been years since I have thought of this.
How yesterday you came to me at dusk
in the bathroom as I was sitting down to pee.
Saying nothing you pulled my head to your belly,
held me there. Saying nothing
you stroked my head, my hair.
Over and over you said nothing.
And from some great dark place, the urine came.

Switchback

Railway Fires Coalmen, Replaces Steam with Diesel
  —Montreal Star, October 1949
Computer, Says Railway, Saves Manpower Hours
  —Montreal Gazette, January 1955

Dad, they are burying you this morning.
For you the rabbi chants *yitgadal vayit kaddash shemay rebah.*
It is not your daughter who reels inside grief, the hole
freshly dug and larger than the one waiting in the grass.
I did all that years ago when you left. Where did you go
when you sat, wood, in the white wooden chair
and watched your garden die? The onions,
rutabaga we seeded, the corn you measured my years by,
the worms I dug, packed in tins for our Saturday morning fish.
Where did you go, night of the coal fires, your hand I lost
to the crowd, a ring of men shouting *down with diesel*
faces above me coming apart like wheels, steaming.
And years later, when the company moved out all the desks
but yours, stacked them like totems in the hall, switched
from papers and eraser dust to one ceiling-high computer?
When did you start needing vodka to feel tall?

The Only Jews in Seredna

for Bessie Weisman Payne, and her father, Abba
Weisman, Seredna, Russia, 1908

They sat for their picture on chairs in the field.
They wore Sabbath clothes.... Jews, a soldier
on horseback yelled, then dragged them
through stones to the street.

She died before I was old enough to ask her
the questions women ask of each other,
Bessie, my grandmother

whose gravestone turned black a year after
she slipped under it with one leg and a pinochle deck

whose words cracked English and Yiddish and fell
to my arms like a bandaged doll

whose cabbages grew pots
on both sides of the ocean

whose mouth never brought me the boat trip back
to Seredna, with Sammy, my father, not yet three

whose father measured barley and beans
and sewing thread, and beat her for leaving

whose back turned from her father to mine
playing with coins *they click like teeth*

who beat him terrible
and afterward cried

whose one leg has resurfaced
in mine, its spidery branch

Catwalk

Across this heavy belly of night
I sputter lightning.
Stand aside, you clawless sleeper.
Curl no longer around stars
pretending to be sight.
Across this fur tongue
I ignite morning,
banish darkness from the balance of my lives.

The Trouble with You

You're always trying to say something, he said. *Lighten up.*

I'll go light, try to get past this. I started with balloons,
black ones, three for a cent. They turned colors as I blew.
I put a few mouthfuls in, pulled them out red, then yellow, finally white.
I tied them flying the phone wires to my belt, walked easy on Mill Street.
I found butterflies, purple, in the punk store, next to the hair gel.
They were reading Garcia Marquez; wouldn't you know it,
I couldn't get them to leave. They'd just read the part
about Remedios The Beauty ascending in sheets to heaven.
I bought the book and turned the page. They followed me
out the door. I was getting this down. On my way home,
I screwed lightbulbs into the street between broken white lines.
I replaced the steel of the train with its whistle.
Flatcars floated inches over the tracks. I looked underneath.
That's when Old Marge, kneeling on concrete on the other side,
pointed to her mouth, asked me to turn to egg whites.

The Box

The box sat on the chair. Metal.
Black. It once held the papers:
birth and marriage certificates, wills,
passports, photos, our wedding, the kids
in the snow, in the mud, in the bath.
One afternoon, when I came home from school,
David was as he was
when he left for work this morning: in his suit,
tie and loafers, a toothpick in his mouth.
His beard beginning to gray nicely.
His leather briefcase bulging with legal briefs.
But that night, when I kissed him hello, the stiffness
around his shoulders tasted of metal.
When he changed into his sweatsuit, I was sure.

There had been signs. Six months ago,
I had returned to school. Walked down
to the university, checked myself in.
I need help, I had told them.
They showed me the library, the stacks,
the classrooms, the coffeeshop.
They gave me a library card,
a number. The questions took time.

When the first one came, it was changing itself.
For example, *when is a wife not a mother?*
became *when is a mother not a wife?* became
what is woman? The question was bright red,
had a smooth shape, carried light in it
if I held it at a certain angle.

The air was crisp; my eyes flushed with climbing
into this new idea. I brought the question home
and placed it on the kitchen table. I fussed with it,
added lemon, and set four place settings.

Where is dinner? asked David,
after he'd changed into his sweatsuit,
opened the mail, and straightened his papers
into six piles. *What is this?* asked Sara.
Pass the salt, said Josh. *Come on, everyone,
this is good. Try it,* I said. *What's wrong with
the kind of dinner we always have?* asked David,
holding his stomach. *I won't eat this.*

That's when the noise began. A knocking.
A quiet tinny knocking. I went to the stove.
The lids were on tight. I looked in the cupboards,
the drawers. Nothing moving. I looked under
the table; the kids weren't kicking each other.
On the table, the question had dried at the edges
of its lemony sauce. I froze it for later on that month.

I brought home more. *How is red?*
Whose turn is it to wash the tub?
What was your mother like, David?
What do you mean, where are your socks?
David tried to unhook my questions
with his *Where is dinner?* He was beginning
to rant. *Don't you learn anything at that school?*

I piled questions not very precisely wherever
I could find a space. I defrosted old ones
and piled them on top of others. There was less
and less room in the house. I began to seed
from books I borrowed from the library.
They began growing into the walls, under the sofa,
in the breadbasket, up the stairs. I resorted
to throwing open windows and piling them
on ledges, hanging them from planter baskets.
The knocking grew louder.

David brought home huge cans of white paint,
spent his evenings running the brush methodically
over each question. Then, he would stand back,
pick up a fresh toothpick, admire his work,
and say, *There. That's better.*
Then, he would come to bed patting his stomach.
And in the morning, his ranting would begin again.
The fresh paint had rolled itself
back down the walls and lay on the floor.

We continued this see-saw for weeks:
he painted at night, and ranted at dawn.
I planted anywhere, found space
where there had been no spaces: on David's
tie rack, in my box of shells. Under Sara's
microscope, among Josh's records.
The kids began to enjoy finding them.
It was a game. After school, they'd rush
to their room, *What'd you get? I'll trade you...*

The house changed shape.
Questions lying on their curved spines
rocked back and forth and encouraged
the perpendicular walls and ceilings to rhyme
with their shape. The house was becoming round.
How is red? became *Red is seventeen,*
forty, passion, chili, blood.

What was your mother like?
became a problem.
It grew an echo and repeated itself
in every room in the house.
The tinny knocking grew louder.

David began to complain about his stomach,
a scraping kind of pain, sharp

like teeth. That's when he started
collecting angular objects, filling shoes
with stones, cigar tins with paperweights,
desk drawers with golf balls.
He took to stacking them
in neat piles next to the bathroom sink.
One morning, he began to swallow them.
One at a time, each with a large glass of water.

No use. Mother was coming up. That night,
about two a.m., the box stumbled out of his sleep.
It floated out, rose above the bed and hovered.
It was still floating in the morning,
but David wouldn't see it. *What box?*
There's no box, he told me.

He started talking in his sleep, sitting up in bed,
his back and legs at precise angles. His lips
snapping open and shut. He talked about
the box he had locked and padlocked
when he was sixteen. With his mother inside.
She had left home, had folded and packed
all her unanswered questions and left.
Walked down the stairs and then down the street.
David had run after her, grabbed her arm,
grabbed her around the waist
of her black Persian lamb coat,
stuffed her into his box.
Padlocked and swallowed her down.

The morning I left, David was sitting on the chair.
His mouth clicked open.
I could see his tongue, black, its tip metal.
I could see his mother inside.
Tiny. Still wearing her coat.

Late Poem for David

From the dark, old wounds cry,
remembering the cleansing.

All these years, silence
has been our momentum,
unspoken words
like a swing pulled back

What I Tell My Son

for Michael

Suppose I drop a mountain on all the numbers
that tie our lives together. The one hundred
and eighty-six the numerologist found in our names,
the twenty-two we found in years by ourselves,
the five thousand seven hundred and forty-eight
if I go by Jewish time and why not.

There's more. Ten inside the phone, four on the doorplate,
nine in the ones supposed to keep us socially secure.
Add in doorplates and phones from twelve other houses
wandering their numbers like tribes through our lives.

Now suppose I drop a mountain on all these numbers.
Or just strip them from their line-up, from years
tied together by mathematical rope, and cereal dust.
Suppose I wrench them from sequence.

Will they implode like black holes? Will they
suck in whole sidewalks and doorknobs,
ceiling walks and night fevers, missing buttons
and beeswax, coal bins, cellar doors, and rain gear?

And where will it all go?
It will whirr behind the clock
that runs backwards at world's end.
It will add itself to the lava
living under my valves since the divorce.

Re-Vision

They came back
to me in a dream
the night after I left:
a long hall, a window
at the end, my father
walking toward me,
his eyes blanked with cataracts,
my mother beside him
and a little to the side,
she was limping,
my brother stiff
in a three-piece suit
and me, surprised,
walking toward them
carrying paper towels
one in each arm
like scrolls

TWO:
SPEAKBODY

...not in words but in moments like this, / bodies within body...
— "Mother Tongue"

Speakbody

If not for her skin, you might be able to see it, the itch.
It pulls her fingers to scratch the back of her knees,
the underhair of her neck. It draws them to her skin in a circle dance
that will not end. She is released when she lets blood.
Since the first night she stained sheets, they have tried to get word to her,
guided her nails to scrape long lines in her flesh. Even the air around her,
like sandpaper, leaves behind fine dry scales of herself.

Today she hurries home, two flights of stairs, spreads a white cloth
on the desk. She smoothes it, unwraps a small blade.
She pulls the zipper down the back of her blouse, lifts it over her hair.
She steps from her skirt, kicks off sandals. Somewhere, a cat.
She fingers the blade. *Pain that has floated me,* she says,
and the radio beside her wafts in and out of stations.
She runs a fig opening across the edge of her belly,
slips the blade along her breasts, between them
to her neck, across her shoulders, around her waist.

>Mouths on her grow in rows, their tongues budding.
>*What took you so long,* they say. She leans closer.
>She cuts her thighs to the knees, steps from the topskin of her legs,
>down both arms to the elbows, her back sliding off in one piece.
>She hangs the skins like blouses to dry.
>She runs the blade sideways to her hips, pulls—

Moons that have entered her body each month now rise.

Drumskin

a red bird searches its own nest
in sheets stretched across the yard

and I stretch skin I've peeled from my body
across circles of wood, lash strips
through holes I've bitten,
pull it taut. I slip down my bandana,
let my hair fall loose between my knees,
and the drum of all my years
like gravel rolling downhill, down
through caves carved (when?) in my bones

who screams using my voice

we move slow as grass
what do you use to stop our coming,
everytime you know before you know you know

Mother Tongue

for Ali

Once, at the beach, I stretched out
on my back, hands pressed to belly
as water lapped my legs
with shells and leaping fish.
I felt you move inside me
for the first time: your legs, your arms,
braille stuttering across my palm.

It seemed the hum of the ocean stopped,
and I was slipping into another time,
a time as a child, when they called me,
drew me to the dining room, to its circle of mirrors,
one on each wall. I'd pull over a stool,
climb up, see myself repeated infinitely.
I'd touch the glass wherever it held my faces.

That day at the ocean, my blood lit with you
inside me, I could see in my infinite mirror:
I'm a caravan of people traveling sand together,
I'm the sweat of a stranger's child in fever,
the sleepless eyes of a friend
packing her son's bag for war,
the ancient chant of a rabbi
uncovering the mirrors of the dead.

Ali, I've been a foreigner on this shore.
I've lost my mother tongue.
Yet sometimes it floats back briefly
not in words but in moments like this,
bodies within body
unslipping the knots.

Los Desaparecidos

Las madres of Plaza de Mayo in Buenos Aires
parade every Thursday in front of the
Presidential Palace, hold photographs
of daughters, sons, grandchildren
who have disappeared.

Like the mother of Plaza de Mayo
I can't put out the fire of disappearing.
On Fifth Avenue, next door to the Guild Theatre,
the man who blankets his child with newspaper,
sleeps in the crawl space of an apartment building.
He turns his face from the blade of light
thrown by patrons opening the theatre door.
They don't see him.
The woman whose feet ulcer from walking the night
on Washington Avenue hurries behind a wall.
In a house on La Mesa Boulevard,
a young girl who won't eat
sharpens her bones the color of fine blue china,
crawls under the tombstone pages of a fashion magazine.
On Ocean Beach Boulevard, 7-11 shoppers
see an old man with three coats stalling death,
sleeping on the heat exhaust
of an ice-making machine. In Argentina
and El Salvador, uniformed men
in jungles and in office buildings might laugh
at the fine way we mask mutilation. No death squads,
no white handprint warnings on doorways here.
No lye poured over bodies to make bones vanish.
In my city the *desaparecidos* obligingly
make themselves disappear.

Signals

> *I have been standing all my life in the*
> *direct path of a battery of signals...*
>
> —Adrienne Rich, "Planetarium"

I.   Two hundred and forty-one
Marines, dead in Lebanon.
Blood from their mouths
doesn't soak the morning paper
or collect indelibly
under our fingernails.
Two or two hundred or
two hundred thousand war dead—
still we don't understand.

II.   You come to me,
my beautiful daughter,
soft from sleep.
You don't understand this war.
I can't explain. Last night
we stood at the sink
washing from sheets
the new blood
that stirs you each month,
promising life.

Back

Beside the old highway, a barn.
I have been here before.
I have never been here.

The smell of scattered hay,
light slashes like steps across the floor,
the smack of loose wood against wood in wind.
I am back
Back
out of reach like a dream
banished with waking.
Morning light enters roof holes,
fingers an old quilt,
a broken suitcase, a brush,
particles of hay tossed.
A woman has been here,
blood and water,
birth in the barn.

Joshua

I could hold you, Joshua,
in the palm of my life
cup my forty years
around your hanging flesh
and say *what have we done.*
I could hold you,
say *you are not my son,*
hold you, tell you lies:

that all babies are born, as you are,
bound to breathing machines,
their bodies weighing less than two pounds
small enough to fit a hand

that all babies are born equal
that I can look you in the eye

this is no lie:
that the moon of your birth night
tracked your mother from hospital to hospital,
spilled its cool light on insurance ledgers
weighing your worth

that her fertile heart froze to sand
each time she was turned away

that at twenty, I was a nurse
starched and stupid with notions of night sirens
unloading pain at emergency room doors
as call to care

I hold you, Joshua, in my palm,
your chest blows, its walls rumble

Sachna

In *Sachna,*
figs hang quiet as tongues.
North of Jerusalem,
I swim in slow turquoise water
and the rushing stops.
Water so clear
I can see my feet.

And in the field, kibbutz
children climb army tanks
painted playground blue.
Their teacher sings to them

coocoo ree coo, coocoo ree coo, tzaylee avodah

an Uzi at his waist.
One boy the age of my son
rushes to hold it,
try his fingers on steel.

In the Year of Asherah

*"For about six centuries..."—from the 12th century
B.C...."down to the destruction of Jerusalem by
Nebuchadnezzar in 556 B.C.—the Hebrews
worshipped Asherah...."*

—Raphael Patai, *The Hebrew Goddess*

She is released from clay, the tall woman,
different from Rilke saying Rodin cracked man
from marble. And so it is she returns,
a Monday in May. Seven mimosa trees
around her, bursting extra flowers. The snake
beside her, re-wondering the world. Purple

as plums, purple as pedagogy, purple
blood spills her vulva, her right hand.
My name is Asherah, she says. Her back is tree
bark, her legs wide-rooted earth. She returns
to herself: a grove of seven women. Returns, turning
the sixth millenium. Her hands naming her kin:
Gaia, Isis, Kali, Yanyatu Elima, Ishtar, Inanna,
The Erased Ones. *How are the children*, she asks.

Ruth

for Ruth, who survived Auschwitz

It's not the length but the height of your days
and how much you could fill them with,
grabbing life between wars like a hungry child
who steals from a plate and runs.

You had envisioned death to be large like you
to be loud to be lion to be late
but it came disguised as a friend since birth.
It was *mayim*, it was water, it was life.

Ruth, we've walked the desert
since you drowned at Eilat,
our mouths thick beneath our feet.

We've brought back your memory,
bleached Masada.
We've brought back your memory
like the sun gaining weight as it climbs.

It's not the length but the depth of time since
your death and how loud your echo
running in cisterns underground.

In the Country of Women

I have been a woman stuck in my own vagina,
wearing glasses, the lens broken,
my face bloated, straining to get out,
the walls around me raw fish

I can see the cuntry of women:
a bus, its windows lighted,
women's faces inside, bloated,
brilliant, laughing.
Its engine shifts uphill.
Two windows are dark
like eyes, slits

I see women near the station,
on the platform, a circle of women throwing
lines of light. They arc
to the left, these lines of light,
now to the right, this is
some kind of weaving

I see the table is set
shafts of red wheat on a plate

I see light around a large hole,
teeth set along the edge,
the light is fire.
Women stand the rim.
They're carrying hoses
that spray fire, they're aiming
the mouth of the hole, the walls
are clay, they're sealing walls,
this will be someone's home,
they live underground

Fish Talk

And it is not known whether my body is flesh or fish...
—Taliesin riddle, Welsh, 13th century
translated by Lady Charlotte Guest, 1848

Twelve fish mouths sat in an egg carton
exchanging stories oblivious to the loss of their bodies,
their heads. Only the flies knew for sure and got right on
with the necessary call to a feast. The storytelling
drew a crowd, some fresh from dental school intrigued
with exotic mandibular formations, others interested
in the language of fish. One story goes that for thousands of years,
fish skins trembled messages to each other through water.
From the first moment a line dropped down, divided water,
hooked a mouth, messages began to lose volume.
Fish found it necessary to swim closer to each other to hear.
Lines continued to fall from skies like a network of nerves.
Silent the skins. Fish flesh fell away from disuse, floated
up to the surface in pieces. Mouths grew muscled,
now gone to the hard hook.

Parturition

I swam in the Dead Sea, salt as hands beneath me.
I had driven the jeep one hundred kilometers into the silence
of the Negev desert to climb a mountain. I walked up clay as sun did sky.
Sweat, salt, the hands under me. Halfway up I found damp caves
and climbed into the dark belly of the mountain, sat on cool black stone.
Two-thousand-year-old Hebrew carvings on the wall: this was Herod's
mountain, built as his safe place. I sat deep in cisterns hollowed
to hold flashwater. I was there five minutes. I have been there
forty years. Today cisterns under my cheekbones fill with quiet.
A body welled in damp purple caves moves its head in me.

Simply

I say *cat cat*
and she pushes her head
under, lifts my arm.
I say *what
do you want?*
Her eyes endless meadow.
She turns over
belly open belly
her paws white flags
to say
love me.
I scratch breathy fur,
crawl inside
her closing eyes,
lie down in grass.

I say *cat cat
come teach us,
hold a seminar,
a world-wide
symposium.
Lift our arms.
Come teach us
open belly.*

Underground

Nine o'clock somewhere near
Victoria Station. No moon. The clatter
the call of wheels of a London subway
pulls me two at a time down black steps
to the underground. Time to go home.
People are standing against tile walls,
sitting on benches. Many of us settlers
from the colonies. Women in veils, women
with stars painted on their foreheads.
Men and women in suits. Men whose hands
know stone, the cutting of trees.
Beside me, a woman in a sari the color of leaves
nurses her baby. The child is wrapped in soft wool
and a language that fits awkwardly in my ears
and naturally within my blouse.
I remember lips of sweet sucking
that my babies left there years ago.
Eyes of women who work in offices,
who live under veils,
all watch the child, the mother.
The sound of sucking
moves from woman to woman
like the pen of a cartographer.

Blueprint

What does a fish see on the way up
that makes its eyes bulge?

—you asked before you moved
away to school.

I build a house
to hold your hurt, unhealed before you left.
It's made of wood and creaks at night,
hallways hung with lanterns.
We roll the dough straight out,
knead it warm, let pain rise full, and float—
until, sitting in the kitchen booth, elbows close,
we feel the ropes unknot,
your breath come loose.

Housegift

Let go that which aches within you,
that which is stone within you...

—Susan Griffin, *Woman and Nature*

I bring you cartons
carry them up the front steps
stack them high in the living room
I untie them one by one
spill them open like gumball machines out of control
cover the couch the floor the Levelor blinds with laughter
that makes your sides ache your cheeks hurt
and spreads like dust your mop can't reach

What Is It About Hair

Why she looped it, braided it, stubborn silk, black,
who can say, it wasn't like hair, not really.
Watch it wander, deliberate clouds.
At night, untwisting on pillows, sudden
curves, like music. Yes, she can almost hear it.
Morning reflex, braiding her hair, an ancient
dance. *Mirror, my breasts are years and
years of eyes just watching* and when she went to
write down what they saw, her pencil broke and
broke again, carrying contraband.

Not Fisher, nor Fish

Lyme Regis, Dorset, England

Fishers and saltmakers lived in Lyme Regis before
that long claw of old gray wall flexed against the sea. Lyme Regis,
the guidebooks say, built on the most unstable land in Britain.
I know this land filled with fossils.

I know this fisher, dogs at her knees, spreading her nets to dry.
I too have hooked a damp worm up on itself, wired metal through flesh
and didn't flinch. I've netted open-eyed bass into the boat,
flapping in foreign air. I've known my flesh wired on metal.

I know this Cobb, this snakewall sloped into the sea.
It cannot shake my boots. I'm surprised each time the Cobb ends.
I shall go further out to sea, feel it shiver, and not slip.

Today I'm not fisher, nor fish. I'm saltmaker.
I let the dogs run loose.

The Night Sybil Came

I'd been trying to reach my mother. I wanted to talk to her. She'd died
fifteen years before and there were questions I wanted to ask her,
things we women had never asked each other. It's not like I wanted to talk to
    the dead,
it wasn't like that. What I wanted was to have some sort of knowing between us.

It was a Saturday night in Tempe, Arizona, a hot desert night. I sat at my desk,
the windows and doors were open and hot winds pushed the room around.
She came to me, was there. I don't know how I knew she was there. She was
there. I had to get up from my computer, lie down on the couch. I was dizzy.
I felt her as hot winds in light, and a voice felt through my fingers.

Later, I went to my desk, and tried to get down in words what had happened.
I sat there hours. No words came. I left the house, got in my car, drove to the
    art store.
I wanted to put my fingers in clay—I'd never worked with clay before.
Within an hour, how I had experienced my mother was there on the table.

I started with her legs. Clay moved in my hands easily. It was as if I knew
what I was doing, how to sculpt. I formed her/she was forming herself, kneeling
on the ground, her legs under her. She was leaning back on her ankles.
Her thighs were thick, strong.

I found my fingers spreading open clay for labia—large—they extended from
the base of her spine, down to her knees. Round, open, like a satellite dish.
Through the hole of her labia, her clitoris extended out, like the tip of a snake.
And that's how it was, her clitoris extending in through the hole, inside her, up,
curling back on itself, rising up and out her mouth as her tongue, as if her
tongue and her clitoris were one, some long curled snake, and it

thrilled me to think that her/my tongue was *bristling all the way up and down with the same kind of tissue as your clitoris.* And that *your clitoris can taste, speak.* And that *it is through your labia that you experience truths coming in as if through satellite from the world and worlds.* She was telling me this.

I tried then to shape her shoulders, her back, arms, her head, but they kept falling off. *Listen to what you know through your body.* She was telling me this too. She was legs, feet, a large labia, and snake extending from clitoris to tongue. Snake wasn't threatening or dangerous—rather, full-alive vibrant, light,
     continuous, one.

I was then able to write about it. It was as if she wouldn't be translated directly into words, she needed the intermediate state of physical being before she allowed words about her.

I remember as a young girl, growing up in Montreal, thinking the name Sybil odd, even embarrassing, none of my friends had mothers with such a name. I remember bringing my friend Rhona Goldsmith into the kitchen, my mother was rolling dough, her hands white with flour, and Rhona asking me what kind of a name is that. My mother answered, *I think it means onions, onions in Yiddish is Tsibliss.* We looked at each other, Rhona and I, shook our heads, what a name, left the kitchen.

Years later, I remember shaking, reading in a book of myths about Sybil, oracle. Onions? From whom did she get her image of onions? The dead, crying?

Sybil, when she did come, was not crying. Her words came through my fingers, with difficulty—a kind of stumbling spelling at first:

I be Sybil don't stopp down the stairs only down and somewhere
we can take this goplemand, sorry I really here, just playing
my way through, you know, francie, I never really told you
momma I hear you in my fingers, talk to me momma *hello lovey*
how you hated me to call you that, watch the corn boil,
now yes, ask me
what was it mom that kept you from telling me
the traces on us, down our backs, the lines I couldn't see
I saw, francie, and you saw later
come, no words, we walk
this time it's my back garden,
your father, I left him years before I was born
you wanted the truth for years, now you can't write it?

in the writing of it, she came through playing something she called a
    goplemand,
(if someone reading this has ever heard of it, write to me)

it was a stringed instrument, made of skin, strung with traces, as in thin, very fine,
horses' traces, only these used on women. I don't know how I knew this,
but I recognized them when I saw them. I'd known for years they existed, felt
    them
on my back, around my neck, in my mouth, but I'd never before seen them.
Sybil, my mother, had taken them off and made them into an instrument,
was playing them, laughing, singing. How like her to make music of sorrow.
I'd never seen her so happy, so full of herself *Your father,*
I left him years before I was born I wanted the truth for years.

The next day, I had lunch with a friend, and described to her the clay
     womanform
I'd made. I left out the part that it was my mother, I was shy about what had
     happened,
I just told her that I'd created this sculpture, and she said
well you know that's the Kundalini, don't you? Who is Kundalini, I asked,
I'd never heard the name before, and she told me about the Hindu
snake goddess, the female principle coiled in our pelvis,
about Zen meditation and the Kundalini rising from the pelvis,
up into the head, and when she does, it's enlightenment,
a thousand-petaled lotus opening

That's when I knew, that was my evidence for something I'd known
in some form for years: that we *are* all one, that there is a common knowing,
a body of knowledge we all have together, across cultures, across time.
I'd never heard or read about Kundalini before, yet I knew her,
she came to me in the form of my mother—she is one with Kundalini, we are all
     one

Woman, Diaspora

this is another return my body knows
with the force of gravity and its pull

different from my plane landing in Tel Aviv,
the push the lurch of brakes trying to stop
and my heart a topheavy boulder
heaved by the backs of thousands of years
rolling out of me knowing the way

the roads are jammed with women
we are dead and we are living
we've come here listening to our hair

we trail worlds we've left behind, they
have been the distance between us

we carry valises from countries across time,
a diaspora of women scattered from ourselves

we are women returning.

on the mountain rim we see radio towers
wired with hair, lakes are pockets of sapphire light,
are these lakes made of water

we're women carrying torn children
and new scrolls we've written

we merge into one mouth
and roll cavernous from it, our scream
raising the tents of womanhouse

This Reality Is Infectious

I live; I am alive;

take care, do not know me,
deny me, do not recognize me,

shun me; for this reality
is infectious — ecstasy.

—H.D., "The Flowering of the Rod"

It's happening everywhere: my friends bursting from former selves—prickly, purple, radiant—like thistles in the sun. The miles between us. Telephones connect the dots, give shape to this new house we're building: Sandy—once stricken silent as bruised plums, her mother burning her childhood diary *how could you write such things, what if your father found this*—now writes political poetry in Fairbanks, Alaska, sends me purple fireweed, the first plant to come back after a fire. Allison—bent and crying over math books in high school, her father telling her *you'll end up waiting tables*—began the first lesbian sorority, now writes films and comedy, sends laughter from Los Angeles. Jenifer—who lost a mother at fifteen, had a child at seventeen, once hesitant to write, *it's presumptuous to believe I have something to say*—now sends her feminist tracts from Minnesota. Kira—once packed up two kids under two, left when he hit her, defied welfare rules *no school, stay home with the kids*—sends political photographs from Salinas: planes spraying strawberries with poison. And collaborating with Kira: our exhibition of women's faces and stories of child abuse taken down in the Capitol building for the old don't-see and don't-say what we know to be true. It rose in us like frostbite: we're being censored. We called in the ACLU, declared it a First Amendment emergency. Then we hung the exhibition in full. *Poetry makes nothing happen,* Auden said. *Honesty is a violent act,* says Hélène Cixous. We live. We are alive. Do not recognize us. Shun us. See only the back of the tapestry, with strings hanging out.

Friendly Fire

Someone wants to know how I feel about women in war, women in war,
I mean sending women, I mean we're talking mothers here,
some kid if the woman gets shot loses his mother, hey they've been
losing fathers down the tubes since who knows when but what the hell
no one ever sent a father home for the kid's sake, fathers I guess
they figure fathers expendable, send the woman home, have to
take care of our women, send her home, someone wants to know
what I think about women and rape, someone wants, every six
minutes a woman is raped a daughter is raped a wife is beaten every
eighteen seconds, someone wants to know what I think, have to take
care of our women, send her home, what I think, send her home
to raise the kid, the kid they care so much about, the one that will grow
and go to war

Long Road Look

we took it out of a bag,
be bigger than all of us we said,
it wasn't as though we knew
what we were doing
the day a long road look
slipped between us,
what was that,
I asked, *what,* you said,
and it was done, just like that.

Raising the Tents

In the first years of the twenty-first century, it was discovered
that voices, all the unheard ones, didn't die at the end of life.
Instead, they spent thousands of years wandering underground.
Cracks in the earth appeared around the world, geologists were called,
new fault lines named. Voices erupted like small gas leaks.

It was an earthquake like no other. The Pentagon was notified.
Linguists were brought in, recordings made, texts consulted.
Women and men around the world stopped arguing, and waited.
There on the ground cooling and forming, finally,
the broken vocabulary of a lost civilization.

The new translations began. With the fine hand of a watchmaker,
words were threaded by elders into language. Words spoken
by women, words spoken by men, clicked across
in front of each other's eyes like subtitles in a foreign film
suddenly playing everywhere.

Author's Note

My use of right-justified margins is influenced by the ancient Jewish practice of writing and reading Hebrew from right to left. There's a conceptual overlap in this book, of my heritage as a Jew and my heritage as a woman (e.g., "Woman, Diaspora" and the concept of a diaspora of women returning to our country of origin). I've long experienced womanness not as gender but as race, a civilization dispersed, with its own language, history, and cultures. I see women and men as countries, and peaceful international relations flourishing when dominance disappears in favor of wholeness and when difference is valued as richness.

I use right-justified margins when the voice in the poem reaches back into the ancient heritage of women-centered cultures for the energy and vision to re-create her future. The answering voice emerges in some of the poems (e.g., "Speakbody"), appearing in italics, as though a foreign language. In "The Night Sybil Came," there is actual connection between the worlds.

Frances Payne Adler

Frances Payne Adler, poet, teacher, and social action artist, was born in Montreal, Quebec, and moved to the United States in 1975. She teaches in the Department of English at the University of San Diego (California). She received an M.A. and B.A. from San Diego State University, and an M.F.A. from Arizona State University.

Ms. Adler's poetry has been published in *Women's Review of Books, CALYX, A Journal of Art and Literature by Women, Exquisite Corpse, Centennial Review, Bridges, Prism International, Quarry, Women and Politics, Daughters of Sarah, Hayden's Ferry Review, Pacific Review,* and the anthology, *Blood to Remember: American Poets on the Holocaust* (Texas Tech University Press, 1991).

She is co-author with photographer Kira Corser of *Struggle To Be Borne* (San Diego State University Press, 1988) and *When The Bough Breaks: Pregnancy and the Legacy of Addiction* (New Sage Press, 1993). These projects plus *Home Street Home* (1984) and *A Matriot's Dream: Health Care for All* (1993) are also collaborative poetry-photography exhibitions that have been displayed nationally. Ms. Adler received grant awards for these collaborative projects from the James Irvine Foundation, the National Endowment for the Arts, the March of Dimes, the Monterey Arts Commission, Las Patronas, the San Diego Community Foundation, and the Copley Foundation.

Ms. Adler's awards include the Helene Wurlitzer Foundation Award for Artist Residency in Taos, New Mexico; California State Senate Committee Award for artistic and social collaboration; Martha Scott Trimble Poetry Award finalist, *Colorado Review;* National Council of Jewish Women, Los Angeles Chapter, Rose Kreisman Scholarship; and Regents' Scholarship, Arizona State University. *Raising the Tents* was a finalist in the 1993 Western States Arts Federation (WESTAF) Book Awards.

Selected Titles from Award-Winning CALYX Books

The Violet Shyness of Their Eyes: Notes from Nepal, by Barbara J. Scot. A moving account of a western woman's transformative sojourn in Nepal as she reaches mid-life. *(Nov. 1993)*
ISBN 0-934971-35-8, $12.95, paper; ISBN 0-934971-36-6, $22.95, cloth.

Open Heart, by Judith Mickel Sornberger. An elegant and genuine collection of poetry rooted in a woman's relationships with family, ancestors, and the world.
ISBN 0-934971-31-5, $9.95, paper; ISBN 0-934971-32-3, $19.95, cloth.

Killing Color, by Charlotte Watson Sherman. These compelling, mythical short stories by a gifted storyteller delicately explore the African-American experience. **1992 GLCA New Writer's Fiction Award.**
ISBN 0-934971-17-X, $9.95, paper; ISBN 0-934971-18-8, $19.95, cloth.

Mrs. Vargas and the Dead Naturalist, by Kathleen Alcalá. Fourteen stories set in Mexico and the Southwestern U.S., written in the tradition of magical realism.
ISBN 0-934971-25-0, $9.95, paper; ISBN 0-934971-26-9, $19.95, cloth.

Ginseng and Other Tales from Manila, by Marianne Villanueva. Poignant short stories set in the Philippines. **1992 Manila Critic's Circle National Literary Award Nominee.**
ISBN 0-934971-19-6, $9.95, paper; ISBN 0-934971-20-X, $19.95, cloth.

Black Candle, by Chitra Divakaruni. Lyrical and honest poetry that chronicles significant moments in the lives of South Asian women. **1993 Gerbode Award.**
ISBN 0-934971-23-4, $9.95, paper; ISBN 0-934971-24-2, $19.95, cloth.

Idleness Is the Root of All Love, by Christa Reinig, translated by Ilze Mueller. These poems by the prize-winning German poet accompany two older lesbians through a year together in love and struggle.
ISBN 0-934971-21-8, $10, paper; ISBN 0-934971-22-6, $18.95, cloth.

The Forbidden Stitch: An Asian American Women's Anthology, edited by Shirley Geok-lin Lim, et. al. The first Asian American women's anthology. **Winner of the Before Columbus American Book Award.**
ISBN 0-934971-04-8, $16.95, paper; ISBN 0-934971-10-2, $32, cloth.

Women and Aging, An Anthology by Women, edited by Jo Alexander, et. al. The only anthology that addresses ageism from a feminist perspective. A rich collection of older women's voices.
ISBN 0-934971-00-5, $15.95, paper; ISBN 0-934971-07-2, $28.95, cloth.

In China with Harpo and Karl, by Sibyl James. Essays revealing a feminist poet's experiences while teaching in Shanghai, People's Republic of China.
ISBN 0-934971-15-3, $9.95, paper; ISBN 0-934971-16-1, $17.95, cloth.

Indian Singing in 20th Century America, by Gail Tremblay. A work of hope by a Native American poet.
ISBN 0-934971-13-7, $9.95, paper; ISBN 0-934971-14-5, $19.95, cloth.

Forthcoming Titles – 1994

Light in the Crevice Never Seen, by Haunani-Kay Trask. The first book of poetry to be published on the mainland by an indigenous Hawaiian woman.
ISBN 0-934971-37-4, $9.95, paper; ISBN 0-934971-38-2, $19.95, cloth.

CALYX Books is committed to producing books of literary, social, and feminist integrity.

These books are available at your local bookstore or direct from:

CALYX Books, PO Box B, Corvallis, OR 97339

(Please include payment with your order. Add $1.50 postage for first book and $.75 for each additional book.)

*CALYX, Inc., is a nonprofit organization
with a 501(C)(3) status.
All donations are tax deductible.*

Colophon

The text of this book is composed in Stone Sans.
Composition by ImPrint Services, Corvallis, Oregon.